The Promise of Prayer

By

Jeffrey Erickson

D1707613

Jeffrey Erickson

Prologue

Our family recently went to the Sacred Grove. It was the first time I had been there in my lifetime. I had a very powerful peaceful experience there as I contemplated how sacred the grounds were and the sacred events that took place there.

During our trip we also visited Niagara Falls. Although Niagara Falls is not one of the Seven Wonders of the World, it was a truly spectacular site, and this led to a conversation with my family about the Seven Wonders of the World. While visiting the Sacred Grove in New York we talked about what the Seven Spiritual Wonders of the World might be. Some guesses included The Garden Tomb, the current temples, and Mt. Sinai where Moses saw the Savior. We also collectively decided the Sacred Grove where Joseph Smith's First Vision took place was definitely at the top of the list. I told my family I am certain it is one of the most sacred places on earth. For me that day, the Sacred Grove certainly felt like one of the spiritual wonders of the world.

As we walked through the grove of trees, we encouraged each family member to have his or her own experience. We separated and all took different routes at different times. There were benches throughout the grove, I picked one and sat and prayed and pondered for fifteen to twenty minutes. I felt the overwhelming peace of the grove. I then felt I wanted a more powerful witness and experience. The Spirit whispered to me, "you are not going to have a more powerful experience unless you kneel." I didn't want to kneel as the ground was wet everywhere.

I wandered along the paths and prayed and pondered. I still did not kneel. The ground just seemed too wet and I thought doing so would stain my pants. I also didn't want to do it for show or look weird as people walked by. I finally listened to the Spirit and found a place to kneel on the ground and ask if this grove was where Joseph Smith saw God the Father and His Son Jesus Christ. After a few minutes, a powerful burning in my bosom came. I asked again and the feeling came again. I was so grateful for this sacred experience.

After reflecting on this occurrence, I am amazed at how immediately I received an answer from the Spirit after asking; God is so quick to bless, so quick to answer, and so quick to comfort. I am grateful that He quickly answered my prayer and sent the Spirit to confirm how important the Sacred Grove is to the salvation of mankind. I am grateful that God would share these feelings and answers with me in such a short span of time. God is quick to answer in so many instances and quick to reward us when we pray in faith.

Nephi shared these insights, *"And I, Nephi, did go into the mount oft, and I did pray oft unto the Lord; wherefore the Lord showed unto me great things" (1 Nephi 18:31).* Nephi's doctrine is that if we will go often to the Lord, He will show us great things. I have seen this again and again in my life. I am grateful for the great things I have been shown, felt, heard, and read in answer to earnest prayer.

My hope is that you will see that through prayer, the Lord offers peace, confidence, hope, enlightenment, miracles, opportunities, changed hearts, direction, inspiration, solutions, mercy, and an awareness that God is involved directly and intimately in everything we do. I have learned that we can claim the promises of prayer *daily*.

Dedication

I am grateful to my father in law, Richard Eddy who has always been one to "pray oft" and "pray earnestly".

Table of Contents

The Promise of Prayer

Many years ago, my six-year-old son Tanner was giving me an overview of how he prayed. He was trying to demonstrate how he reverently approached prayer.

He said, "Dad, when the prayer is being said, I just close my eyes and hold my breath."

This book will not be about tips from Tanner on prayer, it will not be about how to pray, or when to pray, or what to pray for. In approaching this topic, I was nervous because prayer could easily be a 1000-page topic. For this book my goal is to concisely remind us of the numerous (not all) blessings, rewards and promises of prayer. Please do not hold your breath as you read this book.

I had a fascinating experience recently as I observed a group of men cutting branches from trees and putting them into a tree branch machine which demolishes the limbs into smaller parts by pulverizing and shooting them into the back of a dump truck. These machines are amazing, but getting the branches through the chute into the machine that pulverizes can be scary. If you ever get your arm or fingers caught in one of the teeth, you are in serious trouble.

I watched one man whose role it was to move the branches far enough into the machine to be chopped and pulverized. He was pushing them into the machine, but the branches seemed to be jammed. I then saw something that horrified me; he put his hand deep into the machine in an attempt to push the branches far enough in to be grabbed by the teeth of the machine. I told my wife to look. She quickly looked and then she said, "Don't watch that." This meant she did not want to watch the man as it seemed far too dangerous for her to watch. He was literally risking his hands and arms to maneuver these branches into the machine. I saw him struggle and make little progress with great effort and risk. I couldn't take my eyes off the scene, nervously hoping nothing terrible would happen.

I then saw something I instantly knew I wanted to write about. He abandoned his fruitless and risky efforts with his hands, and he went to the side of the machine and grabbed a big broom. He took the broom and proceeded to use it to force the branches into the machine. As an observer, suddenly, my feelings of panic and fear were gone. This simple change in approach brought increased results, increased safety, and he achieved what he was trying to accomplish.

In watching this simple occurrence, I drew a parallel to prayer. Prayer is a wonderful instrument God has given us to be more effective, more protected, and to accomplish our righteous desires. Prayer is given to God's children to allow us to see His hand, wisdom, and desires to bless us in our lives. When we do things on our own, without the help of God, we are often unsuccessful. And without Godly protection, we render ourselves less safe and less productive; we seem to do things the hardest and most risky way possible.

When we use the instrument of prayer (much like the broom), we are more effective, more protected, we see greater results, and we realize how powerful prayer can be in our daily efforts. I have learned that the instrument of prayer always brings righteous results. These righteous results are simply some of the wonderful promises of prayer that God grants to us when we obey the commandment to *"pray unto the Father in the name of Christ" (2 Nephi 32:9).*

The promises of prayer are blessings, rewards and opportunities that we simply forget or may not claim for a season. We talk of prayer, we speak of prayer, we read of prayer, we rejoice in prayer, we routinely pray, we speak of its power, but we don't always draw upon its true power and blessings.

There are numerous promises that come from prayer throughout the scriptures. I hope as you read about these tremendous promises you will have a desire *to "counsel with the Lord in all thy doings" more frequently and more earnestly (Alma 37:37).*

Nephi said, *"I did cry unto the lord, and behold he did visit me" (1 Nephi 2:16).* I love the principle and promise that comes from Nephi's words. If we will cry unto the Lord, He will visit us. If we will pray often, He will show us great things. He will comfort us, forgive us, lift us, strengthen us, inspire us, and calm our troubled souls.

As a bishop, my most serious trial came about three years into my calling. I felt—in many ways—like I had been cruising along pretty well when I was abruptly met with a heavy burden. It was a difficult situation that I needed to deal with, but the burden felt extraordinarily heavy. The weight of someone's sins literally consumed and overwhelmed me. For a moment, I remember thinking that the burden of being bishop was something I was not interested in anymore. For a moment, I was ready to be done; I felt spiritually sick. I didn't want to deal with the trials that were coming for this individual. I felt a little like Alma did after observing the Zoramites, *"O Lord, my heart is exceedingly sorrowful; wilt thou comfort my soul in Christ. O Lord, wilt thou grant unto me that I may have strength, that I may suffer with patience these afflictions which shall come upon me, because of the iniquity of this people"* (Alma 31:31).

In this instance, I literally followed the pattern of Alma and I cried unto the Lord for help and for strength. I know this is not always the case, but almost instantly, the Lord quickly visited me. He told me these were His burdens and He would take care of them. After this sacred spiritual visit, my soul felt lifted and the burden of my calling felt lighter. In this situation the Lord had sprinted to my aid in a matter of a few minutes after my prayer.

Peace returned and I knew I could confidently move forward to assist the Lord with this trying situation. He again fulfilled His promise, *"And God did hear our cries and did answer our prayers" (Mosiah 9:18).*

I am convinced that—despite all the pleas and directives from the Lord in the scriptures—we still don't seek His help, wisdom or guidance nearly often enough. We forget that He has promised that He will hear and answer us. Alma's daily directive would be a blessing in the lives of every one of God's children: *"Counsel with the Lord in all thy doings, and he will direct thee for good" (Alma 37:37).*

Why is it so important for the Lord to visit us? We need to feel His spirit, sustaining hand, love, direction, peace, and we need to move forward in His strength. As Mormon testifies, it is a reminder to us of the Lord's plan and goodness: *"And I, being fifteen years of age and being somewhat of a sober mind, therefore I was visited of the Lord, and tasted and knew of the goodness of Jesus" (Mormon 1:15).* When we cry unto the Lord and He visits us with peace, assurance and comfort, we remember the goodness of God.

Here are two verses I love about being visited by The Lord. Nephi exclaimed, *"... I have seen so great things...the Lord in his condescension unto the children of men hath visited men in so much mercy" (2 Nephi 4:26)*. Sincere prayer is a reminder of a merciful God who will visit us when we cry unto Him. The second is: *"And it came to pass that the thirty and first year did pass away, and there were but few who were converted unto the Lord; but as many as were converted did truly signify unto the people that they had been visited by the power and Spirit of God, which was in Jesus Christ, in whom they believed" (3 Nephi 7:21)*. The Lord will continue to visit those who believe and exercise faith in Him, we just need to invite Him to do so.

May our richest experiences in life come from a loving God who desires to visit us as often as we allow Him and as often as we plead with Him for visitation. May He visit us *"in so much mercy."*

Many years ago, in the Hidden Treasure Mine in Tooele, Utah, ten-year-old Josh Dennis visited the mine on a Friday night with his father and their ward scout troop. Upon entering the mine, the troop quickly separated into two groups. Josh told his dad, Terry, he wanted to catch the scouts up ahead, and his father let him run ahead to catch the first group.

Sometime later when the two scout groups emerged from the cave, young Josh was not with either group. The troop organized and quickly went back in the mine to search for Josh. They emerged again and Josh was nowhere to be found. They were not certain if Josh was still in the cave or if he had come out and was somewhere outside. The scout leaders called in Search and Rescue to help them to find Josh as the cave contained dangerous shafts that would be easy to fall into. The troop members even lowered leaders down some of these shafts to see if there was any evidence Josh had fallen. When Search and Rescue got to the cave, they searched the caves through the night and into Saturday morning without finding young Josh.

Soon, word of Josh's disappearance spread and hundreds of people were there that morning to help in the search. Josh's mom found out on Saturday afternoon when she saw her husband, Terry, returning home from the mine. As they saw each other, they melted in emotion. Terry—a man not one to typically show emotion—was devastated and bawling. Josh's local bishop and ward became heavily involved. Josh's parents fasted. The bishop and his wife fasted. I am certain many others in the ward fasted. The situation was becoming worse by the hour. The bishop gave Terry a blessing saying Josh would be found. The Search and Rescue teams spent all Saturday and all Sunday scouring the cave and outside the cave. They marked the areas carefully that they had searched. By Sunday night, there was still no sign of Josh. Fears were increasing and hopes were diminishing.

Monday came and hundreds came again to the cave to help. Searchers had thoroughly searched outside and inside the cave with its many tunnels and passages. It seemed that they had searched every inch with still no sign of Josh. The situation was puzzling and growing more and more desperate with the passage of time.

Many still clung to hope, but Tuesday came and less people showed up for the search as hope was dimming. The rescue team and many volunteers searched all day again. It was on this Tuesday—after nearly five days of searching—that Search and Rescue said that they would have to call off the search on Wednesday. By the end of Tuesday, there was still no sign of Josh. Ten-year-old Josh Dennis had now been missing for four and a half days. By the end of Tuesday Josh's parents' faith was wavering as they began to accept that the cave might be Josh's tomb. Josh's mom called the assistant scoutmaster to speak at Josh's funeral as she began the preparations.

Wednesday morning came and the site was nearly without any volunteers. There were very few people left to search. The bishop and his wife were fasting again. On Wednesday morning, a man named John Skinner came to search the cave. John had recently become active in the church and been sealed in the temple, and he had been praying for experiences to strengthen him. He had come to the cave on both Saturday and Sunday afternoon trying to help but had been turned away. He read on Tuesday that the search would be called off on Wednesday. John Skinner had an impression that Josh was still alive. He showed up at the cave on Wednesday morning.

John Skinner's grandfather had been the superintendent of the mine when he was young and John had spent a great deal of time in the mine. He told the lead man of the Search and Rescue team that he might know of some places in the cave where Josh might be. At this point, there were not many other options. John was allowed to go in the cave with two other Search and Rescue men.

Twenty-three minutes later the three men emerged from the cave and yelled, *"we found Josh and he is alive!"* I cannot imagine the joy those seven words must have brought to all those who heard them. There were so many miracles in Josh's rescue, but let me tell you the one that applies to our topic today.

On the Friday when Josh went into the cave and was lost, he immediately had an impression to stay put and he prayed multiple times. One of his prayers was a plea that he would be found quickly. Josh felt an assurance that he would be found. When Josh was finally found, he thought he had only been lost for a day, and then when he saw all the equipment outside the cave, he thought maybe two days. It had been nearly five days.

Two weeks after Josh was rescued from the mine, he stood up in sacrament meeting and bore this powerful testimony, *"I wasn't alone in the mine. Heavenly Father sent angels to be with me. I didn't see them, but I knew they were there because I was comforted. I would like to bear my testimony.*

I know God lives and that He answers prayers."[1]

Just as Josh testified, I have learned again and again when we pray in faith, God will visit us. President Gordon B. Hinckley said, *"Let us never forget to pray. God lives. He is near. He is real. He is not only aware of us but cares for us. He is our Father. He is accessible to all who will seek Him."*[2] I am so grateful for His accessibility as I have needed it on so many occasions.

A few years ago, a dear friend at work, Vanessa, decided to take the missionary lessons. I was proud of her for her courage to investigate. On the first visit the missionaries taught Vanessa how to pray. Vanessa was in her mid-thirties, but this was the first time she really had prayed in a sincere way that was not just a memorized prayer. For the first time in her life, she really talked to God with an abundance of sincerity. As our loving Father so often does, He rewarded her efforts.

Vanessa had an awesome experience as she felt God was there. She felt that her prayer was heard. Tears came to her eyes as she truly felt the love of God. For Vanessa, it was an extremely memorable and emotional moment. Here was a wonderful daughter of God who finally reached out simply and sincerely after nearly 35 years, and God immediately blessed her efforts and touched her heart by visiting her. I am so grateful for a God who visits us in our needs and desires and rewards our earnest efforts. May you be visited by the Lord and feel His love as you pray to Him.

Pray in Faith

Many years ago, our family was going on a trip to Florida. My wife had somehow misplaced her wedding ring and couldn't find it that morning. We were to be flying out of town later that night for our trip. As the day wore on, amidst packing and getting ready, she grew more and more concerned as she scoured the house and couldn't find the ring anywhere. She rotated between packing and searching all day. By the end of the day she had finished packing but still had no success in finding the missing and precious ring. She was distraught. We finally left for the airport for our trip and she still had not recovered her ring.

Her worries about ever finding the ring deepened. We talked about it in the car and again on the plane. She decided to seek real help; she decided to pray about it. The entire day she had looked but had never made it a serious matter of prayer. She was so busy and so involved that she didn't stop and earnestly seek the Lord's help.

As she sat on the plane, she turned to the Lord regarding her concerns about her missing ring. After a frantic day, now she calmly and earnestly asked Heavenly Father to help her find the ring. As she prayed, into her mind came the thought of our three-year-old son Tanner. She had watched him earlier that day picking up a myriad of things off counters and tables. She then had the distinct thought to look in Tanner's pocket. He was in the seat next to her on the airplane. She reached over and reached into his little pocket and found her precious ring. After an entire day of searching without the Lord's help and no results, the ring was found at 8:00 pm in less than five minutes with the Lord's help. The promises of prayers of faith are miraculous.

In Alma 31, there were some sacred blessings and promises granted to Alma, his sons and his fellow laborers. These blessings were granted, the scriptures say, *"because he prayed in faith" (Alma 31:38).*

What were those blessings? They were blessed that they would not hunger. They were blessed that they would have strength. They were blessed that they would suffer no afflictions unless they were swallowed up in the joy of Christ.

Why is praying in faith so important? There is probably a large list of reasons, and I will try and cover a few besides the reasons listed above. I am certain one is because we acknowledge, as my wife did, that without God's help, we cannot accomplish our desires. Jacob shares a few other reasons, *"But behold, I, Jacob, would speak unto you that are pure in heart. Look unto God with firmness of mind, and pray unto him with exceeding faith, and he will console you in your afflictions, and he will plead your cause, and send down justice upon those who seek your destruction" (Jacob 3:1.)* Here are three reasons to pray in faith: He will console you in your trials, He will plead your cause, and He will help you obtain justice.

I love this story told in a General Conference talk in October of 1999:

Recently my friend Richard came home from work to find a very small girl sitting on the curb in front of his house, crying. He asked if he could help. Through her sobs she explained that she was lost. He told her that this was his house and his wife was inside. He told her he knew she shouldn't go with strangers, but if she felt comfortable going inside, he and his wife would try to find her home. They went into his house, and his wife, Linda, began to console the little girl. "I'm sure you must be very frightened," she said.

"I was frightened," the girl responded, "until I saw the picture of Jesus hanging on your wall. Then I knew I would be safe."3

I have learned—as this young girl stated— the Savior brings safety, consolation and peace. Through prayer, we can access this same powerful consolation and peace through the Savior.

I have seen this consolation come time and time again as we reach out to God in prayer. Remember Alma and his new converts that had it so rough as the wicked priest Amulon became their ruler:

"And now it came to pass that Amulon began to exercise authority over Alma and his brethren, and began to persecute him, and cause that his children should persecute their children.

For Amulon knew Alma, that he had been one of the king's priests, and that it was he that believed the words of Abinadi and was driven out before the king, and therefore he was wroth with him; for he was subject to king

Laman, yet he exercised authority over them, and put tasks upon them, and put task-masters over them.

And it came to pass that so great were their afflictions that they began to cry mightily to God.

And Amulon commanded them that they should stop their cries; and he put guards over them to watch them, that whosoever should be found calling upon God should be put to death.

And Alma and his people did not raise their voices to the Lord their God, but did pour out their hearts to him; and he did know the thoughts of their hearts.

And it came to pass that the voice of the Lord came to them in their afflictions, saying: Lift up your heads and be of good comfort, for I know of the covenant which ye have made unto me; and I will covenant with my people and deliver them out of bondage." (Mosiah 24:8-13).

The Lord has made us a promise that He will console us in our afflictions. This touching story is an example of the peace that we can access in prayer:

One young mother wrote: "When I was 13, I knew my life was not worth living. I was living in an abusive home where there never seemed to be lasting happiness. My two best friends told me they didn't want to be friends with me anymore because I thought I was too good for them, which made no sense but left me feeling completely alone. As the battles in my house continued to rage, I went to my bedroom. I was so scared. I knelt down and called to the one person I still knew I had. I pleaded to my Father in Heaven to somehow take me home. I said, "Father, I need to be with you. I need to feel your arms around me." As I sat crying and quietly waiting in that desperate moment for Heavenly Father's arms to reach down, I heard a voice, "Put your arms around yourself, and I will be with you." As I followed that prompting, I felt Heavenly

Father's love assure me that I could go on, and I would go on and I was not alone.[4]

Nephi also powerfully reminds us that when we pray in faith, God hears our prayers, *"But I, Nephi, have written what I have written, and I esteem it as of great worth, and especially unto my people. For I pray continually for them by day, and mine eyes water my pillow by night, because of them; and I cry unto my God in faith, and I know that he will hear my cry"* (2 Nephi 33:3.)

One of the most powerful examples of prayers of faith being heard is the prophet Alma as he prayed for his son*: "And again, the angel said: Behold, the Lord hath heard the prayers of his people, and also the prayers of his servant, Alma, who is thy father; for he has prayed with much faith concerning thee that thou mightest be brought to the knowledge of the truth; therefore, for this purpose have I come to convince thee of the power and authority of God, that the prayers of his servants might be answered according* *to their faith. (Mosiah 27:14.)* I love that we are not told how long the prayers were, or for how many days Alma prayed, or that he made a deal with God. This verse simply says Alma and his people *"prayed with much faith."*

One Sunday afternoon we were playing together as a family and then we all sat down for a family meeting. At this time, we had five boys. As we sat down and began our family meeting, we noticed our two-year-old Talmage was missing. My wife asked where he was and I said, "I think he is in the playroom." We sent one of our sons to check but he was not there. My wife and I began to search for a few minutes, but we didn't find him. I approached our sons who were playing and I said, "This is serious. Talmage is gone and we can't find him."

They all began searching and the search became more frantic as time went on. I announced to the boys and my wife, "pray while you look." After a few more minutes of fruitless searching, my oldest son Tyler, eleven-years-old, came to me and said, "Dad, we should say a prayer as a family." This was great advice and a great insight from an eleven-year-old, but I didn't stop or heed his desires. In the hurry of the search I didn't want to stop and gather the family. Every searcher was spread out throughout the yard and the house. This was a bad decision, but it was my feeling of the moment.

My compromise was this, I said, "Tyler, let's you and I say a prayer," and so we did. At this point in the search we were both crying as I offered a plea for help. Every boy in our home was now searching the home, front yard, back yard, and detached garage. We had just moved in our house and had a side fence without a gate at this point so we realized we needed to extend our search down the street. I ordered the two oldest boys to get on their bikes and go down the street off the back gate. My wife jumped in her car to drive around the neighborhood, and she was obviously bawling by this time. The situation was quickly becoming desperate.

Again, my oldest son Tyler found me and said, "Dad, I think we should pray as a family." In my increasingly desperate state, I finally realized this was the best thing we could do. Tyler and I gathered his brothers— Mom was still frantically driving the neighborhood— and my four boys and I knelt in the family room and offered a sincere, heartfelt prayer. This was finally a prayer of much faith. I had not exercised much faith up to this point, but now I knew things were bleak and we desperately needed intervention. By this time, I and all four boys were crying as twenty to thirty minutes had elapsed and we had been very unsuccessful in finding Talmage. We had checked everywhere in the house two to three times. We even checked some scary areas like an empty fridge downstairs, in the washers and dryers, and under huge bean bags. It was scary looking under those things as I didn't really want to find him there.

We finished the prayer and then every boy took off in search again. This time, following the prayer, I had the distinct impression to check the laundry room. I had already searched there two or three times. My son Tanner had already searched there as well. It didn't make sense, but it was a definite impression that came from our prayer of faith.

There was an island in the laundry room with cabinets on the front and shelves on the backside. We ran into the laundry room and checked the back side of the island, and there was little Talmage asleep on the top shelf. He had been hiding from us and had fallen asleep. Just as we found him, we received a phone call from my weeping wife. I said, "we found him!" What a wonderful phrase. Emotions changed and we all went from tears to elation. We knelt in prayer again a short time later and expressed appreciation for the answer to our prayer.

There is tremendous power in prayer, but there is miraculous power in prayers of faith. When Enos prayed in faith, he requested a lot of the Lord, and he was rewarded for his faithful requests: *"And it came to pass that after I had prayed and labored with all diligence, the Lord said unto me: I will grant unto thee according to thy desires, because of thy faith" (Enos 1:12).*

On numerous occasions Nephi desperately needed the Lord to answer his prayers. One such instance was when he and his brothers were returning to the wilderness after inviting Ishmael and his family to come with them to the Promised Land. His brothers and a few others were angry with Nephi, and they tied him up to leave him to be devoured by wild beasts. Nephi, as he always did, prayed with much faith, *"But it came to pass that I prayed unto the Lord, saying: O Lord, according to my faith which is in thee, wilt thou deliver me from the hands of my brethren; yea, even give me strength that I may burst these bands with which I am bound. And it came to pass that when I had said these words, behold, the bands were loosed from off my hands and feet, and I stood before my brethren, and I spake unto them again" (1 Nephi 7:17,18).* I testify Nephi and others were men who prayed with much faith and were blessed with wonderful results.

My sons and I had a tender experience one year returning home from our ward father-and-sons campout. We drove a few miles on a dirt road and then hit the paved road when our car suddenly died. I put the car in neutral and attempted to start the car again. The car started three more times, but each time it died. I pulled over and didn't really know what to do. We were two hours from home. I knew we had gas, and I knew the alternator and battery were okay. I didn't know what to do. I got out of the car and told both of my boys to say a prayer. I got out of the car to see if I could do anything or find anything amiss. I was just grateful I knew the engine was under the hood and not in the trunk. I opened the hood and looked around having no clue what I was looking for. I pushed down on a few things in the engine compartment and touched a few hoses, and then I opened the cover of the air filter. I moved things around a little, but I didn't see anything unusual in there so I closed the filter cover again. I jumped back in the car to attempt to start it one more time after a prayer.

I turned the engine over and it started. That was a wonderful sound.

I turned to my oldest boys Tyler and Tanner and asked, "did you say a prayer?"
They both said "yup."

We started driving down the road and Tyler said, "Dad, Heavenly Father really is there isn't He?"

I said, "You bet he is buddy—more than you'll ever know." We drove the rest of the trip safely home.

Two days later, the car died again on my way to work. This time it would not restart. I was less than a mile from home and I had it towed to the mechanic. I received a phone call later that day when the mechanic discovered the car's problem. He said somehow a large leaf had gotten underneath the air filter and the leaf was blocking the air intake and causing the car to stall and not start.

Somehow, jiggling the air filter two days prior had moved the leaf enough to get us home from our campout. In that instance I just did it on a subtle impression and it proved to be a means of returning home.

Finally, Moroni reminded us about the power of praying with faith, *"And may the Lord Jesus Christ grant that their prayers may be answered according to their faith; and may God the Father remember the covenant which he hath made with the house of Israel; and may he bless them forever, through faith on the name of Jesus Christ. Amen" (Mormon 9:37).* May we always remember that lives are changed, hearts are touched, souls are saved, miracles are wrought, peace is given, and strength is granted when we pray in faith!

Pray Always

One of the great two-word phrases in all of scripture is "pray always." I believe these two words are used together at least twelve times in the Doctrine and Covenants.

Why is it such a powerful phrase? Because whenever the phrase is used, it is followed by absolutely wonderful promises. This phrase and its promises should be reminders of some of the many promises of prayer and righteous rewards that come through prayer.

"Pray always, that you may come off conqueror; yea, that you may conquer Satan,

and that you may escape the hands of the servants of Satan that do uphold his work" *(D&C 10:5).* Wow. Pray to be delivered from the destroyer and even conquer him. Through prayer, you will escape his clutches and snares.

"Pray always, and I will pour out my Spirit upon you, and great shall be your blessing—yea, even more than if you should obtain treasures of earth and corruptibleness to the extent thereof" (D&C 19:38). Double Wow. The imagery of being completely drenched with the Spirit is both powerful and wonderful.

I have uttered prayers to have the Spirit in so many instances. I have felt the promise of the Spirit being poured out over and over again. Let me share this very personal experience.

When I started writing the Greater View Series it didn't start out as a series; it was one book. When I went back to my draft with another idea or two, I thought it would be a two or three book series. As I began to pray and write, the Lord poured out His spirit upon me in abundance. Ideas flowed, Book of Mormon principles and phrases and topics came into my mind, and I continued to write and pray and write.

I am certain that over the last year a loving Father has drenched me through the Spirit with recall of verses, ideas, thoughts, experiences, stories, metaphors, and principles. These principles have become absolutely clear to me. I feel like the gates of the Spirit have been opened wide to help me, inspire me, and guide me to write things that may be a blessing to someone. The spirit of writing about greater views from the Book of Mormon has been a wonderful outpouring for me.

I was asked by a friend the other day if I get writer's block, and without even thinking I quickly said, "No." I was surprised the answer came without thinking, but it was true. I feel whenever I pray and write the Lord directs me in a powerful direction. The experience of writing these books may only change one person, and if that person is me, the books and the experience have been successful. I have learned when I pray always and write; the Lord pours out His spirit upon me.

"Therefore, let the church take heed and pray always, lest they fall into temptation" *(D&C 20:33).* What a powerful principle. Praying always will protect you from falling to temptation.

"And they shall give heed to that which is written, and pretend to no other revelation; and they shall pray always that I may unfold the same to their understanding" *(D&C 32:4).* As sons and daughters of God, if you pray always, understanding will be given unto you. The Lord teaches us through prayer and asking. There are so many principles and doctrines that the Lord can teach us if we will allow Him, through prayer and the Spirit.

"Pray always that they faint not; and inasmuch as they do this, I will be with them even unto the end." (D&C 75:11). If you pray always, you will not faint (not weaken, dim or fade.) You will press forward with steadfastness in Christ because you pray always. I also love the promise that if you pray always, Christ will be with you till the end—until the end of your mission, your life, and your eternal life. Praying daily is critical to strength and salvation.

I have observed many elderly individuals in the temple "not faint" as they serve others faithfully with weekly and even sometimes daily temple attendance. These good saints are a reminder to me of the promise of fainting not.

"Search diligently, pray always, and be believing, and all things shall work together for your good, if ye walk uprightly and remember the covenant wherewith ye have covenanted one with another" (D&C 90:24). This promise is combined with other contingencies, but the promise is tremendous; *"all things shall work together for your*

good." That is a promise for the obedient. Prayer is a critical aspect of obedience. If you will seek Heavenly Father frequently in prayer all things shall work for your good.

I had a unique dental experience on one occasion where I saw this promise fulfilled. Many years ago, I had to go to the dental board for a complaint that was filed by the board against me. The board itself had filed the complaint on a charting technicality, and it was not a complaint from a patient. This complaint process was not fun as I had to take a day off and spend half a day sitting in their office. The process involves appearing before a peer review board who evaluates the complaint, asks questions and then makes a recommendation to the dental board for either an appropriate penalty or dismissal.

The peer review committee consisted of two dentists and a lay person. They were to review the case, ask questions, hear my thoughts and feelings, and then make their recommendations to the board. After asserting my claims and reasons why no penalties or punishment was warranted, they seemed to side with me that there was a small honest charting mistake and their discussion seemed to move towards no repercussions. I was grateful for this direction. They reviewed a few more policies and final comments when one of the peer review members said, "I think we need to give him a letter of concern. I don't think there is any way around that." The group then continued more discussion and were about to recommend that I receive a "letter of concern."

A "letter of concern" from the dental board is a recognition that you are not at fault, but you need to be more careful next time. It is a small black check mark against a dentist. I didn't feel that is what I deserved. As the discussion by the peer group deepened, I invited a fourth member to participate in the peer review. I invited Heavenly Father. I began to pray quietly saying, "please, Heavenly Father, I need some help. Will you do something? Can you help, please?"

I don't recall all my exact words, but I know my prayer was sincere, heartfelt, and filled with faith. Just a moment later, one of the dentists on the committee suggested, "I just think we motion to dismiss, and there shouldn't be anything done." Another committee member inquired, "we can do that?" The third member says, "yeah, I guess." Then the motion to dismiss was made, seconded, and it was all over. A month or two later the board dismissed the case as recommended without any other discussion.

I was so thankful for a simple, earnest prayer and for a peer review member's heart that was softened and swayed a vote. I know God listens and influences our prayers, and I know righteous results come when we pray always.

"What I say unto one I say unto all; pray always lest that wicked one have power in you, and remove you out of your place" (D&C 93:49). If you don't want the adversary to destroy your life with the chains of habit or

darkness, pray always. In the Book of Mormon, it promises Satan will have no power over the hearts of the righteous. The righteous pray always.

Let me share this important story regarding prayer and overcoming the effects and feelings that the adversary can bring into our lives and homes. Dennis K. Brown shares this story about his father:

He was not active in the church for more than 20 years. The bishop came to him and asked him if he would visit a young couple in the ward once a month who had just moved in. He was to see if they needed anything. Dad was resentful, but he agreed.

It was a small trailer house and Dad went. He could hear a baby crying and he knocked on the door. A young woman answered the door. She was carrying the baby and it was obvious that she was expecting a second child. It was also obvious that she had been crying. She invited my father into the very small living room, which was filled with undone washing and ironing diapers, towels and sheets. He found a small box to sit on as the young mother began to cry. "I got married far too young. My baby is always sick. I'm sixteen and I'm seven months pregnant with my second child. I'm always sick. My husband works three jobs, and I never see him. We have not been to church. Life is just terrible!"

After a short time, my father left the home. He felt he had made the girl feel uncomfortable and that he had been an imposition. He told himself he would not return. My mother told Dad to call the bishop, which he did. The bishop asked him to return and to visit the woman again the next month and report back to him. The same thing happened again. There was a sick baby, the mother had been crying. And plenty of laundry to do. My father left again vowing to not return.

The following Sunday was a fast Sunday and usually my dad didn't attend church. The only time he would come was when one of his children was blessed or confirmed, and he would stay for the ordinance and then slip out. He would always sit on the back row, which made it easy to slip out. On this particular Sunday, Marcy, my baby sister was to be blessed. The bishop asked Dad to stand in the circle in the front of the meetinghouse. The ordinance finished and Dad realized it would be embarrassing if everyone watched him walk out of the meeting house so he sat down in the front row and stayed.

In the middle of the testimony meeting he heard a familiar voice from the back of the chapel. A young woman began her words with, "I got married far too young, my baby is always sick. I have been sick, and I will be delivering a baby in the next few days. My husband works 3 jobs and I rarely see him." She then said these powerful words, "There have been 2 times in my life when I felt I might do something drastic to myself and my children. Each time, I prayed as hard as I could, and each time the Lord answered my prayer by sending someone to help me. He sent Brother Brown." As a result of this experience my father became active in the church.[5]

We find tremendous protection from the adversary when we pray always.

I have briefly reviewed a few powerful promises about one phrase: "pray always." There is truly something wonderful about prayer. I don't know if it just because it is a commandment of God. I don't know if it is because we acknowledge God when we pray. I don't know if it is because prayer causes us to remember Him. I don't know if it is because we can draw upon the powers of heaven when we pray. I don't know if it is because revelation comes after prayer. I am not certain of all the "why's" but I know praying always works. For sons and daughters of God who desire to "pray always," the richness of heaven will be poured down upon you and you will truly be filled with the blessings of God.

Consecrate Thy Performance

President Hinckley shared this powerful analogy many years ago:

I hold in my hand a small package that I bought in Switzerland. Do you remember the movie Sound of Music, with its final, beautiful song, "The Edelweiss Song"? It speaks of the flower of the Alps- "small and white, clean and bright, bless my homeland forever."

This is a package of Edelweiss seed. The seeds are tiny, like small dry flecks of pepper.

But on the face of the package is pictured what they might become-the mature plant, the flower that grows high in the Swiss and Austrian Alps, that weathers the storms that rage through those mountains, that blooms beneath the snow, that gives beauty to Alpine slopes and meadows. These tiny seeds have within them the potential for vigorous and beautiful life. They have become the symbol of a sturdy people- *"small and white, clean and bright," blessing a great land forever."*[6]

I have learned that we— like the seeds spoken of—need a loving Father to oversee our growth. We need someone who will plant us, nourish us, fertilize our lives, strengthen our character, sustain us through adverse conditions, and constantly help us grow. One of the great promises of prayer is that God will consecrate and magnify our lives allowing us to become something wonderful and remarkable.

A few years ago, as I read the Book of Mormon, I recorded hundreds of the promises

I found in the record. There were many about prayer, but there were hundreds more regarding other principles. I was amazed, as I am certain my list was not very comprehensive, but it was filled. We believe in a God of principles with promises. As I recorded promises I discovered there are numerous principles I had never thought about, and I can be blessed for living them. Here is a promise about prayer that made an impression on me in family scripture study. It is one "undiscovered promise" I feel that applies to the promises of prayer.

"But behold, I say unto you that ye must pray always, and not faint; that ye must not perform any thing unto the Lord save in the first place ye shall pray unto the Father in the name of Christ, that he will consecrate thy performance unto thee, that thy performance may be for the welfare of thy soul" (2 Nephi 32:9).

Following these words Nephi tells us what he has written is of "great worth." This is certainly a verse of great worth. The last two phrases in this verse are my points of emphasis in the verse. When you pray with power, then comes the huge promise, "he will consecrate thy performance." What does that mean?

Will God make me better at my occupation? Will God help my teaching in church be more Spirit-filled? Will God bless me in my relationships with more love? Will He fill my mouth with the words I should say? Will He help me pronounce more powerful priesthood blessings? Will God give me impressions on what I should do with my life? Will God help me become more disciplined? Will God help me break a habit which is holding back my spiritual progress? Will He help me listen to the Spirit and heed His promptings? Will He help me be a humble servant? Will He help me in my calling? Will He help me with my children? Will He help me with my friends? Will He help me have more courage? The answer to all the above questions is: Yes, Yes, Yes!

Consecrate is an insightful word. What does it mean? It means He will bless, sanctify, make sacred or make holy your performance. I testify God will do that as you pray always. He will consecrate your performance. You will feel, see and know there is a difference when you pray more earnestly. Through prayer, God will magnify your righteous desires and efforts.

Let me share one more simple example of God magnifying our efforts by helping my family and I make it to an important family event. We were flying to Utah one day at 4:30pm for a family baptism. This was very important to us and I was to get off work early and meet my wife at the airport. Everything was going to go as planned. At about 1:30 my wife called me at work frantic and said the flight was actually departing at 2:30. We had made a serious mistake in our planning. My wife hadn't finished packing and I was still at work. I still remember her saying, "we will never make it." It was important that we made it so we both hurried. Someone at work covered my remaining patients and, somehow, she threw everything together and left from home. For her the airport was at least twenty minutes away with no traffic, and for me a little less. I wanted God to somehow consecrate our efforts to make the flight. When I jumped in my car to head for the airport, I had a small request. I prayed that God would make our plane late so we would somehow have time to make the flight. I was selfishly not worried about the other 180 passengers. It was truly looking impossible for us to make the flight and the event.

As I was running to the gate with literally no time to spare, I glanced up at the flight board. With my quick glance at the flight departure board I saw one flight was delayed. It was our flight. There may have been more delays, but I only saw one. I immediately expressed my gratitude and arrived to the gate, where I was united with my frantic wife and family. What an answer to a simple man's prayer. The flight ended up being delayed a half hour. This was sufficient time for us to make the flight and attend a wonderful family event in Utah.

I learned a few great lessons from this experience. The Lord cares about the little things in our lives. If you will ask in faith, the Lord will deliver. I also learned to be specific with the Lord. We might have only needed twenty minutes, but I was grateful for the thirty. I was also very grateful no one was praying for the flight to be on time as that may have thwarted my spiritual efforts. I feel the Lord blessed our efforts that day.

The promise is that He will "consecrate thy performance" for the welfare of your soul (and for the souls of others). As you pray for a consecrated performance, may you turn your life over to God and watch as He changes your heart and mind and sanctifies you and blesses you more than you ever dreamed.

I work a few days each week with a wonderful nurse anesthetist named Maureen. She is talented and does an amazing job putting children to sleep for dental procedures. I have worked with her for over 20 years and have been blessed by her excellence in her occupation. She is remarkable at starting IV's on patients.

Occasionally we have a difficult patient where no veins are visible, and after an attempted stick or two no IV is obtained. In these instances, there is concern about not being able to place an IV for emergency medication and sedation medication.

Every time Maureen faces one of these difficult IV placements, she prays and she tells us she prays. She then invariably is able to find a vein and place an IV. I am thankful to work with such a wonderful lady, not of my faith, who knows that God will consecrate her performance even in her occupation.

Years ago, when Agnes Bojaxhiu (Mother Teresa) made the decision to become a nun, her brother presented some opposition. Lazar, her brother, was serving in the Albanian army, when he wrote to her and challenged her decision. She wrote this reply to him, *"You think you are important because you are an officer serving a king with two million subjects. But I am serving the King of the whole world."*[7] Always remember whom you are praying to and serving— the King of the Universe, and He will consecrate your performance if you will ask Him to.

Here is a powerful approach used by a pilot during a very difficult situation. In 1989 Dave Cronin was flying a big 747 on the second to last flight of his piloting career. He had just left Honolulu and was heading to Australia on United flight 811. Suddenly, on ascent at about 22,000 feet, a forward cargo door blew out resulting in a huge hole in the side of the aircraft. This disaster resulted in two rows of seats and nine passengers being ripped out of the airplane. Immediately, two of the plane's engines became inoperable. Dave was in a bad spot, but there were 328 other passengers and 15 flight attendants still on his plane, and he needed to act quickly but decisively with skill and precision.

Dave carefully turned the plane around and somehow safely landed the plane preserving the lives of the remaining passengers and crew. After safely landing the plane Dave was asked how he coped with the trying situation. He said, "I prayed and then went to work." Dave also said, "There is no way I could have brought the plane down without God's help; if I had made one wrong maneuver, we never would have made it."[8]

I am grateful in my life for pilots, leaders, parents, a good wife, and for all those who have prayed and then went to work in my behalf. I know the Lord has consecrated their efforts. I am grateful for a Savior that pleads with us to pray and go to work. May we fervently pray and go to work assured that God will consecrate our efforts.

Conclusion

Mormon observes that the people of Helaman received these blessings from prayer: *"Nevertheless they did fast and pray oft, and did wax stronger and stronger in their humility, and firmer and firmer in the faith of Christ, unto the filling their souls with joy and consolation, yea, even to the purifying and the sanctification of their hearts, which sanctification cometh because of their yielding their hearts unto God" (Helaman 3:35).*

The scriptures reveal to us this list of blessings that have been bestowed through prayer. The list is extensive as it goes on and on. Here are some promises from prayer observed in the scriptures: ministering angels, the outpouring of God's spirit, baptisms granted through repentance, the spirit of prophecy, the spirit of revelation, mercy, peace, protection from entering into temptation, strength, and deliverance from enemies.

I have a dear friend I will call Cliff (name changed). I spent a great deal of time as a bishop attempting to activate Cliff and his wife. In time he and his good wife came back to church. They felt the Spirit and were blessed with church activity. It was amazing to see their progress and the change in their lives. It was wonderful. Cliff eventually received the Melchizedek priesthood. They were preparing for the temple, when they suddenly quit attending church. I believe Cliff forgot about the blessings and promises of prayer. Suddenly, he was reading material from people who hate the church and the restored gospel. In time this affected him as he forgot the source of all truth is God and not men filled with hatred and vengeance. Soon, Cliff was posting his newly discovered positions of anti-Mormonism and his disregard for church authorities.

I watched Cliff's life spiral downward. He began engaging in a variety of sins that he had previously given up. All the peace, prosperity and progress he had made was lost. His marriage suffered, his kids suffered, his life suffered, and his testimony was neglected and destroyed. If only Cliff would have just remembered one simple promise of prayer from the Lord: "But ye are commanded in all things to ask of God, who giveth liberally; and that which the Spirit testifies unto you even so I would that ye should do in all holiness of heart, walking uprightly before me…doing all things with prayer and thanksgiving, that ye may not be seduced by evil spirits, or doctrines of devils, or the commandments of men" (D&C 46:7). Cliff's life was decimated by doctrines of deception, and blessings he had obtained were forfeited.

We are also given these powerful admonitions regarding prayer: *"Pray much"* *(Alma 45:1), "pray oft" (1 Nephi 18:3), "ye must pray" (2 Nephi 32:8), "pray always" (2*

Nephi 32:9), "pray continually" (Alma 13:28), "pray without ceasing" (Mosiah 26:39), "pray in your families" (3 Nephi 18:21), "pray steadfastly" (3 Nephi 19:30), "pray vocally" (D&C 19:28), "pray earnestly" (103:35), and "pray everywhere" (1 Timothy 2:8). We must never stop praying, and we must never stop seeking wondrous blessings through prayer.

Here is one blessing I received through prayer that I will never forget. A few years ago, I was doing a dental procedure on a patient and I was removing a few teeth. I had done this procedure many times before without incidence. It was rather routine extractions on the lower jaw. On this particular day I was extracting teeth on an older lady, and this is what occurred without being too graphic.

I removed her front teeth on her lower jaw and was contouring the bone in the area, when suddenly, blood started shooting out from this area of the mouth. Somehow, I had hit a little arteriole in her bone and it was pulsating every time her heart beat. At first it was a little embarrassing as my staff had never seen this before, but I quickly realized I must get the bleeding stopped. I had seen this in a residency and I felt I knew what I needed to do to stop the bleeding. I first tried simple pressure with gauze and it didn't work. I tried this a time or two and it was unsuccessful. I then used the next means I had been trained to use to stop bleeding, which was cautery. I attempted to cauterize the arteriole with a hot instrument. I put pressure on it and then quickly cauterized, but the fluid was coming so fast the cautery wasn't working. When I released the wound each time the blood would squirt across the room again and again. I battled this problem for nearly ten minutes (it felt like two hours). I am certain I attempted to stop the bleeding arteriole at least 10 times, without exaggeration.

I could see the impending problem. This woman was frail and sleight of frame and it would not be long before her loss of blood would become extremely dangerous. I finally turned to my Father in heaven. I stopped what

I was attempting to do and said a prayer, "Heavenly Father, please, I need Thy help to get the bleeding stopped. This lady is in danger." My prayer was sincere, it was simple, it was desperate, but it was filled with faith. I then proceeded to do the exact same thing I had done ten times before, using a cautery instrument. This time when I removed the cauterizing instrument, I released the pressure and the bleeding was no longer squirting. The bleeding had stopped. I was grateful, but also amazed that I had failed ten attempts at stopping the bleed without the Lord, and with one attempt with the Lord, I had succeeded. I was so grateful that day for prayer, for faith, and for a loving and merciful God who answered my prayer so directly and so immediately.

Nephi encourages us who are on the fence of prayer: *"And now, my beloved brethren, I perceive that ye ponder still in your hearts; and it grieveth me that I must speak concerning this thing. For if ye would hearken unto the Spirit which teacheth a man to pray, ye would know that ye must pray; for the evil spirit teacheth not a man to pray, but teacheth him that he must not pray"* (2 Nephi 32:8). May you never forget this promise to those who use the power of prayer: *"And if ye are purified and cleansed from all sin, ye shall ask whatsoever you will in the name of Jesus and it shall be done"* (D&C 50:29).

May we have the same righteous rewards that Jacob did who said: *"Now, this thing was pleasing unto me, Jacob, for I had requested it of my Father who was in heaven; for he had heard my cry and answered my prayer"* (Jacob 7:22.)

May we live as Amulek suggested when he said: *"let your hearts be full, drawn out in prayer unto him continually for your welfare, and also for the welfare of those who are around you"* (Alma 34:27). As you do this, you will observe righteous rewards and see the promises of prayer fulfilled in your life.

Notes

1. Carolyn Goates Campbell, "Hidden Treasure: Ten-Year-Old Josh Dennis Lost in Mine," *Ensign*, Aug. 1991.
2. Gordon B. Hinckley. *Standing for Something.* New York City: Three Rivers Press, 2000.
3. Virginia U. Jensen, "Home, Family, and Personal Enrichment," *Ensign*, Nov. 1999.
4. Janette Hales Beckham, "Making Faith a Reality," *Ensign,* Nov. 1997.
5. Dennis K Brown. *Evidences of the True Church.* Bountiful: Horizon Publishers, 2002, p.138.
6. Gordon B. Hinckley, "Watch the Switches in Your Life," *Ensign,* Nov. 1972.
7. Kathryn Spink. *Mother Teresa—A Complete Authorized biography.* New York: Harper One, 1997, p.11.
8. Guy Clifton. Oct. 6, 2010. "Dave Cronin, hero pilot of United Flight 811, dies at 81 in Minden." Retrieved from <https://unitedafa.org/news/2010/10/6/dave-cronin-hero-pilot-of-united-flight-811-dies-at-81-in-minden/>.

Acknowledgments

I am certain I could not have written any of "The Greater Views series" without the promise of prayer. As I write about the wonderful principles of the gospel of Jesus Christ I am blessed with ideas, verses, quotes, insights, impressions, and stories that support what I am trying to write about. As I reflect on topics, I am amazed how a loving Father allows me to come across information, read stories, apply personal experiences and read talks that directly apply to the principles I am writing about. I would be amiss if I did not recognize how instrumental prayer is in this process. With no intent to praise my writing, I often look back at what I have written and realize those ideas did not come from me, but from the spirit of God as a result of prayer.

I have felt the promise prayer in my life: I have lived what Nephi taught when he said: *"I, Nephi, ...having great desires to know of the mysteries of God, wherefore, I did cry unto the Lord; and behold he did visit me" (1 Nephi 2:16).* I have been visited by the Lord through his spirit time and time again through prayer and it has changed my life.

I am grateful to Holly Banks for her diligent efforts on improving and revising the manuscript.

I continue to be amazed and grateful for the Book of Mormon and the thousands of principles the Lord teaches us through its pages. I am also grateful for the deepened doctrines, principles of power and the greater views which the Spirit shares with me on a daily basis as I study the contents of the greatest book on Earth.

About The Author

Jeffrey "Jeff" Erickson has been a youth speaker at Especially For Youth (EFY) for over fifteen years. He has served faithfully in many capacities in the church including gospel doctrine instructor and bishop. He has a passion for writing and speaking about the gospel of Jesus Christ.

Jeff is one of the co-founders of NSFC (Non-Sunday futbol club) Arizona. This three-year old soccer club is the first non-Sunday competitive soccer club in Arizona.

He is the recent author of the powerful missionary resource <u>A Weekly Letter to Your Missionary</u>. He is also the author of the first thirteen books in *The Greater Views Series;* "The Fourth Nephite Effect," "The Symbolism of the Sixty," "A Voice of Thunder," "Shake the Chains of Sin," "Waterproofing Your Vessel," "End the Conflict of Decision," "Perfectly Honest," "An Eye of Faith," "Standing With Power," "The Crime of Contention," "The Right Way," "The Virtue of the Word," and "The Arms of Safety."

As a young man, Jeff served a full-time mission in the Canada Halifax Mission. Jeff and his amazing wife, Christine, have six sons and one daughter and reside in Gilbert, Arizona.

41159775R00047

Made in the USA
Middletown, DE
04 April 2019